WISDOM - UNLOCKED

Akhil Ramaswamy

Think Tank
Books

Title: Wisdom Unlocked
Author: Akhil Ramaswamy
First published in 2021 by Think Tank Books
Address: RZ-26/27B, Ashok Park, West Sagarpur, New Delhi - 110046
Website: thinktankbooks.com
Email: editorial@thinktankbooks.com

ISBN: 978-81-947561-4-9
Price: INR 180/-
Maximum retail price of this book listed is only for the Indian subcontinent.
Selling price may vary elsewhere.

5 4 3 2 1

~~~Acknowledgements~~~

I thank my parents Smt MVL Kameswari and Sh NG Swamy for giving me this life to experience it and also supporting me during ups and downs.

I have no words to express gratitude to my friend Sh Anil Kumar Rajagiri who has stood with me at all times and motivated me to push myself to achieve bigger things.

This work could not have been possible without the support from my spouse Smt Satya Anusha.

I finally thank all the people and events that have been a part of my life which ultimately aided in generating thoughts on various aspects of life.

I am indebted to my publisher, Gaurav Sharma who runs the publishing house - Think Tank Books for agreeing to publish my work.

Last but not the least, I thank my friend Ms Shreya Agrawal for introducing me to Think Tank Books.

~~~About the Author~~~

Akhil is a passionate investor in capital markets. Biographies of great achievers and leaders who transformed the course of history in their lifetime have always been an inspiration and motivation to accomplish something massive in one's lifetime.

Akhil also has a love for entrepreneurship and carries the sole vision of building a great investment company in the years to come in order to serve millions through employment generation, building infrastructure and charity. He has special leaning towards teachings of spiritual Gurus and possesses an urge to understand the reasoning behind practices and principles of different religions and cults.

The present work is an outcome of the author's self quest to comprehend the meaning of life and various things that happen in it.

LEADERSHIP

1. Leadership is exhibited by displaying empathy but not by showing sympathy.
2. The effectiveness of a leader lies in directing the energy of his followers towards a unified objective.
3. He is the leader who lives for his people rather than for himself.
4. Loyalists to a leader are like pillars to a building.
5. Leadership lies in organizing the disorganized mob.
6. A leader is the one who makes his vision as the vision of many.
7. Unconventional thinkers become leaders. Conventional thinkers become followers.
8. Domination is trying to keep everyone under you while leadership is taking everyone along with you.
9. A leader inspires courage but not fear among his men.
10. You win people with empathy but not with authority.
11. Doing good is important but stopping bad is also equally important.
12. Character of a Leader is reflected in his people.
13. Anarchy happens in a nation when the leadership of that nation is unable to show proper direction to its people.
14. Presidents and Prime Ministers are marketing agents of their nations.

15. There is always an unending debate on centralization and decentralization of power. It's the conflict between freedom and control.
16. We have experts to offer advice but we need leadership to implement it.
17. Behind the rise of a great leader, there are sacrifices of many men.

FAITH & RELIGION

1. If a religion takes the path of extremism or fanaticism, it fails to obtain social sanction.
2. No one has the right to enforce their religion on others. It's up to the people to accept or reject it. Affinity towards a religion should happen naturally.
3. All faiths are different rivers joining the same ocean.
4. Religion loses its meaning if the people who follow it, don't follow Dharma.
5. Religion came out of Dharma; it's not Dharma that came out of religion.
6. Pain, anger, hunger, heat, cold, happiness, sadness have no relation to any religion.
7. Religion has the power to convert a lifeless object into a power centre.
8. What's the use of religion when people keep fighting in the name of it?
9. Religions and sects are created to control and bring order in society.
10. Traditions are expressions of gratitude.
11. Religion is used as a weapon to gain control over the masses.
12. Purpose of customs and traditions is to promote discipline, health and biodiversity.
13. Traditions should liberate but not confine an individual.
14. There is no religion bigger than wealth & power.
15. The fight between Dharma and Adharma is eternal to keep us busy.

LOVE & HATE

1. Humans unconditionally accept and love themselves.
2. A person loves himself more than anyone else.
3. The biggest investment in any relationship is time.
4. No one loves you more than yourself. Now stop wasting time trying to get the love of someone else.
5. You love someone because the feeling of loving someone is giving you happiness.
6. I have no time to hate others as I am too busy loving myself.
7. You hate others when their behaviour is not according to your expectation.
8. People who love you will never leave you in spite of misunderstandings.
9. Love for others is temporary whereas love for the self is permanent.
10. If you wish to maintain a relationship, then remember only the good things that happened between you and the other person.
11. You have tongue to praise but not to abuse. You have hands to help but not to harm. You have a heart to love but not to hate.
12. When faith exists between two individuals, all kinds of suspicions are reduced to ashes.
13. Expectations have no place in love. If you have them, it's not love.
14. Accepting the other person as they are is love.

15. Acts of violence originate from fear and insecurity. Acts of love originate from courage and belief.
16. When you hate yourself, you begin to hate others. When you love yourself, you begin to love others.
17. When you cannot be yourself in a relationship, it is bound to fail.
18. No two are the same. We have differences of opinions. It's not forgetting those differences that makes a relationship stronger. Celebrating those differences makes a relationship stronger.
19. Argument is useful for lawyers. But for others, it drains time, energy and strains relationships.
20. A relationship is at its best when we respect each other's space.
21. Relationships are best tested during the times of difficulty.
22. Relationships are based on trust but not on doubt.
23. For a relationship to sustain, it should be bereft of expectations.
24. It's easy to win but hard to sustain. It's easy to destroy but hard to create. It's easy to fall but hard to rise. It's easy to hurt but hard to make anyone happy.
25. Small acts of love, few words of appreciation and small acts of gratitude convert a relationship into a lasting one.
26. Love should be natural and unconditional. It should not be filled with demands and expectations.

27. Sex is fulfilling when union of minds happen and not just the bodies.
28. Love should inspire trust and courage but not fear and suspicion.
29. It's not just affinity but trust that forms the basis of any relationship.
30. Love has no barriers. Love is unconditional and universal.
31. Differences of opinion are common. Conflicts arise when we are not open to such differences.
32. Love is all about giving and expecting nothing.

LIFE IN GENERAL

1. In the process of abusing others, we abuse ourselves.
2. If you don't have patience, you will become a patient.
3. We keep hearing that Money is the root cause of all evil. But lack of money is the root cause of misery.
4. Money is the universal religion. It can break all barriers.
5. One virtue is enough to make our life great. It can be patience, discipline, integrity or anything.
6. Thinking differently is the precursor to progress.
7. Not pursuing one's passion is misusing one's opportunity to live.
8. People always come up with one or the other reason for not doing something. That's why the majority remain poor and only a few become successful.
9. As parents, one should ensure that their child becomes physically fit, mentally tough, intellectually strong and morally straight.
10. Selfishness is the core nature of every human.
11. Circumstances don't control you. It's your reaction towards them that decides your future.
12. Fate of a person lies in his speech.
13. The weak keep expecting the help from others. The Strong help themselves.
14. Always be away from doing what is wrong and always be ahead in doing what is right.

15. There are many things in life on which we cannot reach a consensus.
16. Suicide is the worst and physical exercise is the best way to express frustration or depression.
17. Appreciate the greatness of a person when he has the necessary merit even if he is your opponent.
18. Observation is a great teacher. We can learn many things just through our observation.
19. It's hard to reach the top. It's harder to remain on top.
20. Many people value money more than time and end up losing both. If you value time, you end up gaining both.
21. Disasters and crises make people of all categories come together.
22. It's a crisis that drags people into revolution.
23. A revolt is a manifestation of prolonged suppression of frustration and suffering.
24. Respect the person who tried and failed than the person who failed to try.
25. Hard times create strong men. Strong men create good times. Good times create weak men. Weak men create hard times. It's a Cycle.
26. A farmer is a soldier inside a country who takes care of food security.
27. Habits are powerful. They have a compounding effect on our health and wealth.
28. The regressive and conservative approaches always hold us from progressing in life.

29. The weak always need someone to blame.
30. Anything is best understood when done practically.
31. Your time is limited. Fill it with happiness.
32. There is no medicine more effective than a happy mind.
33. Time is the only precious thing in life as we cannot get back the lost time.
34. Politics is all about few persons trying to gain control over the system.
35. Life is temporary. We need to remain happy and fearless and do what we love.
36. Seasons keep changing but the sky remains. Waves keep rising and falling but the ocean remains. Successes and failures keep happening but life remains.
37. The thought to create or to destroy something originates from the same mind.
38. Large goals demand large sacrifices.
39. Each person has his or her own set of problems to fight.
40. The real fight is within you and with yourself.
41. Any technology or a system that promotes freedom is bound to thrive.
42. As how day and night have an equal role in sustaining life on earth, people and their representatives have an equal role in sustaining a democracy.
43. Both problem and solution go together.

44. Anger leads to wastage of energy and destroys peace of mind.
45. Never forget the help done to you by others.
46. No two are equal. No person is inferior or superior. Each person has his own sets of strengths and weaknesses.
47. Never confuse ego with self-respect. Ego destroys an individual whereas self-respect builds an individual.
48. Too much of anything is detrimental.
49. Only those who have the courage to try unconventional things, create history.
50. If few people fight, it's an agitation. If millions fight, it's a revolution.
51. Unpredictability is the spice of life.
52. A lie is like a fire on the match stick. Truth is like the light of the Sun.
53. Equality cannot be achieved in totality. Differences are bound to remain.
54. A person is happy when his passion and profession are one and the same.
55. There is always a difference between existence and living. Pursuing one's passion and having a purpose forms the basis of living.
56. If you believe something, it exists. If you don't believe something, it doesn't exist. Your belief determines the existence or non-existence of a particular thing.

57. The best business in the world is to mind your own business.
58. The food we consume, the events we see, the sounds we hear, have an influence on our thinking.
59. The world around you changes as per your thinking.
60. Rivers are the lifelines of civilizations.
61. Distribute the strain to reduce the pain.
62. The journey is always more fascinating than the destination.
63. A man without an occupation and passion is like an impotent.
64. Power lies in anonymity but not in publicity.
65. A reliable enemy is far better than an unreliable friend.
66. You cannot win the war just because you are on the right side.
67. If terrorism is an external threat, corruption is an internal threat to a nation.
68. Half of our lifetime is spent in sleep.
69. Great people don't give a damn to petty things.
70. Strength of a person lies in making friends but not in creating enemies.
71. Create fear among your enemies and courage among your men.
72. There are two kinds of people who fail in life. Those who don't listen to anybody and those who listen to everybody.

73. Sometimes knowing what not to do is more important than knowing what to do.
74. Too much of tolerance is self-defeating.
75. Charity is good if it reaches the deserved.
76. The eight basic needs of people are – food, water, shelter, health, education, employment and security.
77. Victory and defeat are just two states of the same mind.
78. Sometimes application of violence becomes inevitable to bring order.
79. Petty wars are fought with the fist. Massive wars are fought with the mind.
80. Sometimes it becomes inevitable to lose many battles to win the WAR
81. Real lessons are learnt outside the classroom.
82. An intelligent person is like nuclear energy. He can use his intelligence either in a productive or destructive manner.
83. Nothing can outshine the beauty of nature.
84. Girls disturb the minds of boys with their looks whereas boys disturb the minds of girls with their flattery.
85. Crisis and insecurity unite people.
86. Problems arise when we have too little or too much money.
87. The poor have nothing to lose, the rich have too much to lose. It's the people in the middle who fear the most.
88. Police use violence as license to silence criminals.

89. Police are the fire to create terror in the minds of criminals.
90. There is no rowdy bigger than police if they start using all their powers.
91. Reserve love for few and fear for many to get things done.
92. Sometimes wars are the investments made by corporations to capture the market or resources.
93. Under the influence of lust, one commits blunders.
94. People who complain the most are the people who suffer the most.
95. People get united when they are in the minority. People get divided when they are in the majority.
96. Everything has two sides… that's the beauty of life.
97. Kilometers of proverbs are easy to utter. But it's tough to put them into practice.
98. The rate of growth of the difference between the rich and the poor is directly proportional to the crime rate.
99. The Internet is an ocean of knowledge. It's usefulness depends on the user.
100. The Internet is the democratization of knowledge.
101. People forget the differences between them when they have a common problem.
102. Poverty spreads like a communicable disease in countries infested with terrorism.
103. Higher the poverty, higher the crime.
104. A Law without enforcement is like a mouth without teeth.

105. The business of selling damage and death is Insurance.
106. A road without speed breakers and a relationship without quarrels are boring.
107. Never show mercy on the person who doesn't deserve it. If you show it, you need to feel sorry for yourself.
108. Festivals are celebrated to upkeep fraternity and biodiversity.
109. Acquired knowledge gathers meaning only when it is utilized.
110. It's the dedication and focus of the student which motivates the teacher to bless him with knowledge.
111. While delivering justice, one shouldn't spare even one's kith and kin.
112. Nature takes care of itself.
113. None can challenge nature's fury.
114. Life is an unending learning and unlearning process.
115. Each person develops his own set of beliefs and perception about the world based on his experience.
116. Your perception is your reality.
117. The more one tries to control nature, the more aggressive it becomes.
118. If the burgeoning population is not provided employment, demographic dividend will turn into demographic liability.

119. A person's innocence doesn't give you the right to exploit him.
120. Never judge a person by seeing his status in the society.
121. People fight on some issue when they are bored with the routine of life.
122. Self-defeatist strategies are innovated under the influence of anger.
123. Obstacles expand mental horizons.
124. Don't try to define anything. If you try to define something, you are restricting the scope of it.
125. Old structures and institutions collapse to make way for the new ones.
126. Mind pollution is the source of all kinds of pollution.
127. Acid rain is God's urine on mankind for polluting the planet.
128. A body develops fat and iron develops rust when unused.
129. Lamenting about the past is a waste of time.
130. We should not worry about the past as we cannot change it. We should be optimistic about the future as we can create it.
131. All the problems arise because no two think in the same way.
132. We have mountains of grains but millions hungry.
133. The best weight reduction formula – burn more calories than you consume.

134. All great people have a common habit – they read a lot.
135. Great thinkers create a world within themselves.
136. Scold in private and praise in public.
137. Life without challenges and news without controversies is boring.
138. Each one feels that he is correct in his way.
139. No two persons are alike. It's death that makes everyone appear alike.
140. Humbleness of a person is tested when one becomes successful.
141. Don't disturb and get disturbed.
142. Our mood changes according to the sounds we hear.
143. Each person develops his perceptive based on his experience.
144. It's not the age but the character that inspires respect.
145. Two schools of thought – means justify ends & ends justify means.
146. If there is no struggle in life, then there is no life.
147. In a struggle you should be prepared to see blood and give blood.
148. Mammoth projects have mammoth gestation periods.
149. We study history to prevent the mistakes committed by our ancestors and to imitate their good practices.

150. People in the east get attracted to the logic of the west... people in the west get attracted to the traditions of the east.
151. Anything in excess loses its value.
152. There is no point in crying after someone dies as they are not going to come back to life.
153. When the state fails in its duties, charitable institutes take birth and gain prominence.
154. People marry to obtain a permanent sexual and emotional partner.
155. Every advancement in science and technology brings with it both positive and negative utility.
156. Time is the solution to problems which don't have timely solutions.
157. Some are born to follow; some are born to lead while some are born to be independent.
158. Even when a celebrity goes to shit, that news becomes a hit.
159. Death of millions keeps happening to ensure sustainability of life.
160. People worry about posterity and neglect their present duty.
161. A burning issue loses fire when a new issue crops up.
162. There is a day and night difference between preaching and practising.
163. People who worry the most are the people who suffer the most.
164. More the unemployment, more the anarchy.

165. The toughest job in the world is to sit idle.
166. Every person is a book. You get to learn something new from every person.
167. Nature often keeps reminding humans of its presence to keep his ego under check.
168. If you are busy running behind temporary gains, you will miss permanent gains.
169. Every morning we get up with an intention to become better than yesterday either on a materialistic plane or spiritual plane.
170. People think too much and make things complicated.
171. Life is an opportunity to apply the power of reasoning and discrimination to serve the world at large.
172. Freedom has been the centre of all conflicts. People fight either to gain freedom or to preserve their existing freedom.
173. Trying to tamper with freedom leads to conflicts.
174. Medicines should be produced to cure diseases. But diseases should not be created to sell medicines.
175. Freedom is the most craved privilege.
176. Every human wishes to exercise one's freedom of thought and expression. In the process of exercising one's freedom, one should not infringe upon the freedom of others.
177. Beauty lies in innocence but not in appearance.
178. Uncontrolled passion is madness.

179. There is no medicine bigger than rest.
180. Proper sleep prevents anger and ensures digestion.
181. Planting a sapling is not enough. Ensuring its growth is equally important.
182. Life without freedom to exercise one's will is equal to death.
183. People think and act in an ordinary manner but expect results to be extraordinary.
184. When your job doesn't excite you, you become a liability to your organization and to yourself. When your job excites you, you become an asset to the organization and to yourself.
185. Technology helps in good governance as it improves accountability.
186. We have too much of motivation but too less of implementation.
187. We are experts at analyzing others than ourselves.
188. Intelligence of a person can be gauged from the way one applies knowledge.

IT'S ALL ABOUT "YOU"

1. Don't become someone else's time pass dude.
2. Investing in yourself is the best investment you can ever make.
3. You always keep fighting an unending war within yourself.
4. There is no point in wasting time and worrying about things that are beyond one's control.
5. It's your mindset that determines who you are and who you will become.
6. Only few deserve goodness and respect. If you show it to undeserving people, you will end up getting exploited by them.
7. A person's strength of character is directly linked to the NO he says to things that are not in agreement with his conscience.
8. The power of belief is highly magnetic. Initially there can be no one supporting your stand. As you stick to your stand and work towards your goal untiringly, people automatically get attracted to your sphere of influence.
9. Self-education is the best education. When others teach you, they bring in their conditioned thinking. When you learn by yourself, you will develop your own intuition.
10. One should be oneself and not change for others.
11. Who can be a better guru than yourself as you know about yourself more than anyone.

12. You need PDF to achieve anything – Passion, Discipline & Focus.
13. You will always be happy if you take everything that happens to you in a positive way.
14. If you don't like the person you see in the mirror, it's time for change.
15. If you start reacting to minor criticisms and petty issues, you will lose focus on the ultimate target.
16. Preparation without a target is the same as undertaking a journey without knowing the destination.
17. Hatred thrives on consumption. It either consumes you or the person you hate.
18. Underestimating yourself is the greatest crime you can inflict upon yourself.
19. Let people think what they want to think. But you do what you want to do.
20. People who understand you, will never leave you and those who misunderstand you, cannot be stopped from leaving you.
21. Anything may happen to us. What's more important is how we react.
22. Fill your mind with positive thoughts and shut all the negative vibes.
23. You are the outcome of the thoughts that are manufactured inside your brain.
24. You need to be extremely passionate and intensely focussed on your goal and achieve it with sheer will power.

25. Take out time for yourself. Question yourself as to what drives you, what gives you happiness and satisfaction, what gives you a sense of completeness and achievement.
26. The process should give you happiness, not just the result.
27. You are already great. You need to believe it and realize it.
28. Your luck begins to unfold when you face a crisis as you will get to know the true nature of the people around you.
29. You rise from good to great when you follow your passion.
30. Life becomes monotonous when you fail to identify as to what drives you.
31. This is all you need – a life without fear, regret and dependency.
32. The level of success you wish to attain is proportional to the sacrifices you need to make.
33. Your life is the manifestation of your thoughts. You become what you think.
34. You are not defeated unless you accept defeat.
35. The best comes out of a person when one pursues one's passion.
36. Just follow your conscience as what you feel is right and wrong is relative.
37. Don't waste time worrying about what's right and what's wrong. If you waste it in a dilemma, you end up accomplishing nothing.

38. Frame your own set of beliefs and just do what you intend to do.
39. When you are not happy, you cannot keep others happy.
40. When you cannot help yourself, you cannot reach a position where you can help others.
41. Everything starts with you.
42. Don't expect sympathy or help. Just get up and move on.
43. You are bound to achieve what you intend to achieve if you possess unwavering faith in yourself.
44. You are lucky when you face hard times. Hard times turn you into a person of steel.
45. It's only during hard times, you get to know your true potential and your true friends.
46. Belief makes a common man produce uncommon results.
47. Detachment is one of the most essential traits which one needs to develop. If you are attached to something, you will do anything for it by breaking the ethical barriers.
48. It's better neither to get addicted to anything nor to get attached to anyone.
49. Your birth doesn't make you great. Your acts and thoughts make you one.
50. No person is inferior or superior by birth. It's their conduct that makes them one.
51. When you don't implement what you say, you don't have the right to say.

52. If you don't like something, don't complain. Complaining leads to hatred and frustration. Come out and show the world what you can do.
53. Frustration comes when what you love and what you do, don't match.
54. Life is the only chance to be all that you can be.
55. You have both strengths and weaknesses. Focus on strengths and eliminate weaknesses.
56. The only way to get rid of stress is by doing what you feel like doing.
57. You have infinite power within yourself which needs to be realized and unleashed.
58. A country is said to be independent when it has energy and food security.
59. The harder you work, the luckier you get.
60. The way to learn anything is by doing it.
61. When you love what you are doing, you will become successful by default.
62. Never reveal your intentions or goals till you accomplish them. After accomplishing them, people will automatically get to know about them.
63. Be terribly fast and ruthlessly ambitious.
64. Time is your best friend and enemy. If you make use of it, it is your best friend. If you waste it, it becomes your enemy.
65. Laugh when you lose because you have one more chance to win. Laugh when you win because you have one more chance to overtake yourself.

66. There is no point in saying ALL THE BEST because you have to be the best. If you are not the best, try till you become the best.
67. An enemy is your friend as he keeps you alert and ensures that you keep growing.
68. The best competitor you can ever have in this world is YOU.
69. Help an enemy if he seeks your help as you may be in his situation in future.
70. Win-win is the best way to grow. You grow and help others to grow.
71. Always do what you like the most as you can go up to any extent to achieve it.
72. Real power lies in the mind and not in the muscle.
73. Failure can be written in 3 words – Excuses, Blames and Laziness. Success can also be explained in 3 words – Passion, Discipline and Focus.
74. Work when the world sleeps, so that you can sleep when the world works.
75. When what you say and do are one and the same, you develop credibility.
76. You develop credibility when your actions match your words. You develop a brand when the products and services you offer are consistent.
77. Avoid the company of low thinking people because they neither accomplish anything nor encourage anyone to achieve anything.

78. A man who can control his senses can not only write his own destiny but also change the course of history.
79. Our mind is a reflection of this universe. It's Infinite and ever expanding.
80. You should not speak. Your actions, your results and their impact should speak.
81. Finding your passion is the purpose of your life and living it is your life.
82. There are two kinds of people – those who don't follow their passion and those who don't know their passion.
83. A person who conquers anger, conquers the world.
84. Self-defeatist strategies are innovated when a person is under the veil of anger.
85. Anger destroys you. It's the destruction of anger that builds you.
86. Anger is like nuclear energy. If it's not controlled, the destruction it can cause is immeasurable.
87. No person is going to listen to you unless you prove yourself.
88. Once you succeed, people start coming to you by default.
89. Emotions should not control you. You should control your emotions.
90. Listen more than you speak. The more you listen, the more you learn.

91. No person is an overnight success. It's focus, consistency and never back down attitude that makes one successful.
92. If anyone irritates you, insults you or obstructs you, don't lose your temper and become impulsive. Wait for the right time and show your mettle.
93. Even if you know a lot, keep your mouth shut. The more you open your mouth, the more you are going to invite attention and become more susceptible to attack.
94. Don't imitate anyone. Have your own style.
95. People don't care about excuses and reasons. They care about results.
96. Comparison breeds hatred. Self-assessment leads to excellence.
97. Both hero and villain are inside you. What you decide to become, comes out of you.
98. Each one has his own ways and means to reach their goal.
99. You should be a creator but not a follower.
100. Never hesitate to learn anything from anyone. If you feel shy, you are the loser.
101. The lesser you worry, the healthier you remain.
102. Win over yourself to win over the world.
103. Like how buoyancy keeps the ship floating, belief keeps the spirit of a person floating.
104. The lesser you speak the more peaceful and powerful you emerge.
105. Your way of perceiving things changes the game.

106. When you fail in your attempt, you become the best teacher as you know what not to do. When you succeed in your attempt, you become the leader as you know what to do. What is important is that you make the attempt.
107. Don't give a damn to what others think when you know what you are doing is correct according to you.
108. What is right and what is wrong is a never ending debate. Do what you feel is right according to you.
109. More the obstacles and opponents, more interesting is your journey towards your goal.
110. The more the hurdles one faces, the more one gets to know about oneself.
111. Don't do anything to impress others. Do it only when it impresses you.
112. The decision you make today, determines your tomorrow.
113. None can destroy your self-confidence till you become the destroyer of it.
114. If a lion lives with the dogs, it begins to think and live like a dog. If a dog lives with lions, it begins to think and live like a lion. Your thinking depends on the company you keep.
115. When you stick to your guns, some call it madness while some call it determination.
116. Whatever you speak, determines your wealth. Whatever you eat, determines your health.
117. We step back to kick with more force.

118. Focus is the atom bomb that destroys all kinds of distractions.
119. Focus is saying NO to 99% of things that are unrelated to your goal.
120. Toughened by pain and hardened by obstacles, one becomes a man of steel.
121. Demoralization and flattery are used to defeat an individual. One who guards himself against these two, remains undefeated.
122. It is better to take a decision rather than remaining indecisive.
123. Finish the problem before it finishes you.
124. Your attitude determines your growth.
125. Your growth is limited by your thinking.
126. The occupation you enjoy the most is the occupation that suits you the most.
127. When you are determined to win, who can stop you from winning?
128. Three Ps for success are – Passion, Patience and Persistence
129. When you win, people commend. When you lose, people comment. So, stop thinking about what people have to say about you.
130. When you win, people stand in the queue to take suggestions. When you lose; people stand in the queue to offer suggestions.
131. Your good time starts from the day you fail. When you fail; you get to know your true friends and your true potential.

132. If you are successful, people own you. If you are unsuccessful, people disown you.
133. A person loses when he competes with an intention of not losing the race. A person wins when he competes with an intention of winning the race.
134. Hear what everyone says but do what your conscience says.
135. Be like a magnet attracting knowledge and positive things from different directions.
136. Don't try to rule over someone. Be the ruler of yourself.
137. If you don't focus on your health, ill health will focus on you.
138. Being sceptical about everything you see and hear is a mental disease.
139. One needs to control one's mind before one decides to influence others minds.
140. Your future will be the manifestation of the thoughts that run for maximum amount of time in your mind.
141. When you believe in your vision, there is no need for anyone's sanction.
142. You become what you think about yourself. So think high, become powerful.
143. Don't do something because someone told you to do it. Do it only when you feel like doing it.
144. Solitude is the environment where you talk to yourself.

145. You become wiser by talking to yourself than by talking to anyone else.
146. There is a teacher inside you. Find him, explore him and learn from him.
147. Conquer your mind to conquer the world.
148. Self preparation is the best preparation; self analysis is the best analysis; self motivation is the best motivation. Knowledge of the self is the ultimate knowledge.
149. There are always 2 sides to everything. It's up to you to take the side you like. It doesn't mean that the other side is wrong.
150. Love optimists as they encourage you in achieving your goal. Love pessimists as they challenge you in achieving your goal.
151. When you want something desperately, just believe that you are the person born for it and work for it with a single-minded focus. One day you will be the possessor of it.
152. History is the best teacher. Time is the real opponent. Sense organs are the top distractors.
153. Don't try to change yourself to impress someone. If you do that, you end up cheating not only others but also yourself.
154. Don't do something to impress someone. Do it only when it impresses you.
155. Stop thinking and start doing; stop talking and start doing; stop losing and start winning.

156. If you want to conceal anything, just keep it to yourself.
157. A secret ceases to be a secret even if it is known to a single person other than you.
158. You are unique and you are the salesman for your uniqueness.
159. Success stories teach you what to do and failure stories teach you what not to do.
160. You are your own fan. You are your own hero. Recognize the hero within you.
161. Some take your belief as self-confidence while others take it as arrogance.
162. Never worry about the past as you cannot change it. Never worry about the future as you cannot predict it.
163. Faith in you is the faith of the highest form.
164. The one who possesses perseverance ultimately wins.
165. Freedom of thought is the only freedom which no one can steal from you.
166. Never run behind people who don't care about you. Always take care of the people who run behind you.
167. Even if you are unintelligent, perseverance can take you to tremendous heights.
168. In the process of upholding the truth, you may face many problems and opponents.
169. It's not the dress you wear but the attitude you carry, gives you the style.

170. The sleepless nights you spend in the process of achieving your goal bring endless smiles of happiness after you achieve it.
171. The ultimate way of achieving mental peace – mind your own business.
172. Never complain. Search for solutions.
173. Exercise regularly to stay fit and to get rid of stress.
174. The innocent you are, the purer the smile.
175. Be natural, be original, be yourself.
176. The more you talk, the more you reveal about yourself.
177. The more you become emotional, the more you become vulnerable.
178. The person who invests in himself is the best investor.
179. Silence is the answer to your critics and action is the answer to your opponents.
180. The more you try to run away from the problem, the more it gets compounded.
181. You cannot satisfy everyone. If you try to do it, you end up losing your identity.
182. If you lack interest in what you do, you are bound to fail.
183. If you allow weakness to override you, it swallows you.
184. When you win, people get jealous. When you lose, people show sympathy.
185. A walking elephant doesn't care about the barking dogs.

186. When you win, even people unknown to you start owning you. When you lose, people known to you start disowning you.
187. Lesser the emotions, better the decisions.
188. If you are rejected by someone, rise to a level where you can reject them.
189. Losers give excuses. Winners show results.
190. Take the good in others and neglect the bad in them.
191. A situation becomes a problem or an opportunity in the manner you take it.
192. There is no place for weakness, there is no place for excuses, there is no place for impossibility.
193. You will have no stress when you follow your heart.
194. Prolonged negative thoughts and stress lead to chronic disorders. One needs to stay away from stress and focus on being happy.
195. The more you value every second, the more you stay ahead in the race of life.
196. You keep searching outside for solutions and happiness when both are within you.
197. You are not unlucky when you are disabled. You are unlucky when you lack confidence.
198. If you lose weight, you gain health. If you gain weight, you lose health. If you lose ego, you gain people. If you gain ego, you lose people.
199. Never try to please anyone. Do what you feel is right.

200. Everyday is an opportunity to be better than yesterday.
201. It's the interest that keeps you alert and its disinterest that makes you sleep.
202. When you start seeing good in others, you will start feeling good about yourself.
203. The only person whom you need to ask before you do anything is yourself. Act in accordance with your conscience.
204. You will get what you are destined to get. You will never get what you are not destined to get.
205. In the process of hurting others, you hurt yourself.
206. Sun remains the same whether it is day or night. It's the earth that keeps changing. Similarly people may perceive you differently at different times but you remain the same.
207. Any comment or criticism can disturb you only when you get influenced by it. Getting influenced by it or not depends on your mental strength.
208. Remaining in silence gives peace not only to you but also to others.
209. Your thoughts determine your deeds.
210. Don't do anything to others when you dislike the same being done to you.
211. To accomplish anything extraordinary, one needs to stretch beyond one's comfort zone.
212. Never complain about anything. When you dislike something, either ignore it or try to change it.
213. Never act… be natural… be yourself…

214. If you dislike something, it's better to say NO in the beginning than saying it later.
215. Always stay away from doing what is wrong and always stay ahead in doing what is right.
216. Diseases and depressions come to us to make us physically and mentally strong.
217. Power lies in your attitude.
218. Balance of power is the objective of diplomatic negotiations.
219. You are attacked when you are least prepared to counter it.
220. Emotional people are unfit to rule. People take wrong decisions when they become emotional.
221. If an army of 100 lacks unity, even a minor army of 10 can defeat it.
222. We wish to acquire power to serve the community at large. But the majority of time is wasted in obtaining and preserving it.
223. Life is a golden opportunity to try whatever you want. If you fail to try out of fear, you will regret later.
224. When you want something passionately, nature gives you the power to realize it.
225. Don't waste time on people who don't have time for you.
226. It's tough to say NO. But you should say NO if you don't wish to suffer.
227. By faking you are not only fooling others but also yourself.

228. Why do you need a teacher when you have one within you ?
229. Till you are doing what gives you happiness, you are always rich.
230. To learn more, just listen more.
231. If you depend on others for your happiness, you are bound to suffer.
232. Only when you are happy, you can spread happiness and attract happiness.
233. It's the attitude which makes or breaks an individual.

GOD & SPIRITUALITY

1. Spirituality is not suppression of one's desires. It's the ultimate expression of the soul.
2. What does it mean by being human? In Spite of having an opportunity to harm or punish anyone, you don't do it.
3. The answer to all the unanswered questions is God.
4. People continue to believe and fear God till there are things that are beyond their control.
5. The most commercialized item of present day is God.
6. Even God doesn't pardon you if you repeatedly commit mistakes and confess before him.
7. Whatever we earn or acquire is not just because of our sheer merit.
8. Death is the ultimate reality.
9. Death is the ultimate spiritual teacher.
10. There is nothing more fearful than death. When death is inevitable, what is left to be feared ?
11. The certainty that life offers us is death.
12. Equilibrium state of mind means having the same state of mind during success and failure.
13. Real games happen inside.
14. Every second of your life is uncertain. Just live it to the fullest and fill it with happiness.
15. Faith forms the basis for any religion.
16. Is there a use of any religion or ideology if people fight and die in the name of it ?

17. The happiness we derive out of helping others is the happiness of the highest form.
18. We cannot take back all that we earn. We need to earn plenty and spend plenty of it for the benefit of this world.
19. One should not do things against nature. If we disturb nature, it will disturb us. If we protect nature, it will protect us.
20. The more you try to control someone, the more they try to run away from you.
21. The more you try to control nature, the more violent it becomes.
22. Can you find anyone more loyal than your dog? Can you find anyone who loves you more than your mother? Some things cannot be replaced. They are nature.
23. Real power lies in purity of thoughts and actions.
24. Attachment to detachment is the ultimate attachment.
25. What is the path of truth ? when what you think, say and do are one and the same.
26. God is ideality.
27. A purpose attains purity when it is selfless.
28. Committing acts of violence may give you an instant sense of pleasure but acts of service give you eternal sense of peace and happiness.
29. Everything in life has two sides. It depends on how we see things.

30. Man perishes in the process of acquiring land. But land never perishes.
31. Sometimes, inaction is the best action.
32. Like day and night, a person is a combination of both good and bad in him. It's the conflict between these two, that fills the life of a person.
33. Some believe in the existence of God while some don't believe in it. Whatever may be the stand, "BELIEF" exists.
34. An act of charity is better than a prayer.
35. Every organism has its unique role to play in sustaining life on earth.
36. Your body gets purified with every bath you take. Your soul gets purified with every act of service you do.
37. Preachings of seers of every religion are like colours that make up the white light.
38. The seers of all cults aim at eliminating all the differences. But the paradox is, they end up creating a new cult.
39. People who give adversity to you, aid you in awakening your dormant spiritual power.
40. Adversity is the root out of which the tree of philosophy grows to bear the fruit of happiness.
41. If the knowledge you acquire helps you in becoming more detached to the results of your efforts, it's termed wisdom.
42. Lowest level of living – when you cry at others happiness. Medium level of living – when you

enjoy others happiness. Highest level of living – when you become the reason for others happiness.

43. Problems arise when we have either too less or too much of anything.
44. The fight between what is right and what is wrong always keeps us busy.
45. Life is a 3-D experience. Debts, Diseases and Defeats are essential for spiritual progress.
46. The physically challenged, the mentally challenged, the poor and the aged are the living Gods. They exist so that we can get rid of our sins by serving them.
47. Immortality is the state of the mind whereas mortality is the state of the body.
48. Getting rid of ego is the message of any scripture.
49. Praying god is nothing but invoking the supreme energy that is lying dormant in you.
50. Every planet in Astrology explained in 2 words – Sun is power and vision, Moon is mind and its stability, Mercury is business and intelligence, Venus is beauty and comfort, Mars is fast and furious, Jupiter is knowledge and wisdom, Saturn is law and discipline, Rahu is illusion and unconventional, Ketu is detachment and spirituality.
51. God is the master of the Art of Balancing. He creates both good and bad guys at the same time to keep us occupied.

52. We have two ears. One to hear the necessary and the other to let go the unnecessary.
53. By gaining knowledge, few become arrogant while some become enlightened.
54. As desires increase, stress increases.
55. Lesser the stress, higher the receptivity.
56. You develop stress when you get influenced by what you see and hear.
57. Many fight in the name of faith instead of following the teachings of its founder.
58. When we are drowned in materialism, we forget humanism.
59. Anything under the Sun, living or non- living can be your teacher.
60. Peace of mind can be attained through detachment but not through attachment.
61. Man creates his own problems for his own entertainment.
62. People pray to God out of fear and to fulfil their desires.
63. Ego is a cruel teacher.
64. Ego makes one blind to one's flaws.
65. Prayer is the process of development of self-belief.
66. All "isms" are children of humanism and grandchildren of universalism.
67. Mind without madness, body without deformations and health without ailments are god given assets.
68. All philosophies are different mental speculations.
69. People often crave for what they don't have.

70. The slowest process is creation. The fastest process is destruction. This is the paradox in God's creation.
71. God is generous. He creates all kinds of people to keep the human race busy.
72. There is a supreme energy which is beyond human comprehension and imagination which we call God.
73. There are 2 things – helping others and hurting others. It's your choice that determines whether you are a god or a demon.
74. No belief is absolute and permanent.
75. We bring nothing and take nothing. But we trouble each other for everything.
76. Gods never fight but people fight in the name of God.
77. Fear of god is created to prevent humans from committing atrocities.
78. Faith in god is more powerful than the knowledge of scriptures.
79. God appears to you in the way you wish to see him.
80. Having faith is more important than offering prayers with fear.
81. Some disasters happen to bring about mammoth transformation in the society.
82. Greed turns a man into a beast.
83. A person is happy and peaceful when he has no expectations.
84. Purity and divinity are directly proportional.
85. Lesser the thoughts, better the health.

86. Ignorance is not lack of knowledge. Ignorance lies in thinking that we are creators of our destiny.
87. Dispassion about worldly things makes you passionate about spiritual things.
88. From every happening, there is a new learning.
89. You are a demon when you derive pleasure from others' suffering. You are a human when you sympathise with others' suffering. You are divine when you empathize with others' suffering.
90. Your divinity lies in identifying the divinity inherent in others.
91. Self-introspection leads to self-awareness.
92. Disasters are usually considered unnatural. Disasters are sudden natural events which occur from time to time to restore balance in nature.
93. For every grain of rice we eat, for every molecule of oxygen we inhale, for every drop of water we consume, we are indebted to nature.
94. If you have more than you need, it's an opportunity to help those in need.
95. When you have only compassion radiating out of you, the entire world becomes your family.
96. Eyes are the voice of the soul.
97. Breathe in virtues and breathe out vices. Become healthier and happier with every breath you take.
98. Before we perish, we should give back more than we had consumed.
99. Intentions become pure when they are selfless.

100. Freedom is the inherent natural craving of any living entity.
101. All faiths preach the same but their modes of preaching are different.
102. As a human we have an obligation to make this earth a better place to live before we die.
103. The deeper we think, the lesser we speak.
104. Everyone wishes to remain independent but keep others dependent. This is the root cause of all problems.
105. The air we breathe, the water we drink, the land on which we live have no barriers like region and religion. Then why should we have these differences among us ?
106. Who are you to give and who is someone to take ? It's the god in you that motivates you to give. It's the god in someone that gives you an opportunity to help. You both are his agents carrying out his act.
107. Whatever has to happen will happen when it has to happen.
108. Without individual reformation, we cannot have societal transformation.
109. Anything more than necessary becomes poison.
110. You can neither control your birth nor your death. Do you think you are the controller of your life?
111. The power you acquire, the wealth you earn, the knowledge you gain loses its purpose if it's used for other's detriment.

112. Every human is a combination of both virtues and vices. The objective of life is to maximize virtues and minimize vices.
113. Journey of a person should be from excitement to enlightenment.
114. Conscience is the union of mind and heart.
115. Lover of god never hates anyone because it's the energy of god that is present in everything.
116. Divinity can neither be defined nor imagined. It can only be experienced.
117. Many possess knowledge but only few have realization.
118. Spiritual discourses are not a means of entertainment. They are a means for enlightenment.
119. The purpose of life is to overcome desires and attain the state of supreme consciousness.
120. Expecting others to behave in a matured manner is a sign of immaturity of the self.
121. Falling in the grip of desires is Maya or illusion.
122. Contentment is an attribute of the inner world.

EVERYTHING REVOLVES AROUND POWER

1. Rules are created by rulers to keep people in order.
2. Silence is the most powerful weapon.
3. In the run for money and power, we not only lose our peace of mind but also make others lose it.
4. Power is the responsibility bestowed upon us to serve the community at large. It's not an instrument to suppress people.
5. When the existing power fails to deliver justice, a new power rises to replace it.
6. History is written in favour of the winners.
7. Believe your people but keep testing them without them noticing it.
8. Eliminate all the threats and all the sources of threats.
9. A politician is different from a leader. A politician works for power whereas a leader works for a cause.
10. In the run for power and wealth, man forgot the purpose of his birth. In the process of achieving them, he is digging his grave.
11. You don't need anyone's permission to rule.
12. Democracy and Dictatorship redefined: Democracy – I need your permission to rule. Dictatorship – I don't need your permission to rule.
13. When the bad in this world are united, unity among the good is inevitable to annihilate them.
14. If you wish to change the rules, just become the Ruler.

15. A weak ruler is thrown away by the people. Weak people are suppressed by a dictator.
16. Corruption is the cancer that can make the nation go from rose bed to death bed.
17. It's the hunger for wealth and power that clouds the sense of ethics and justice.
18. Every political party remains clean at its inception. Later, the cancer of corruption creeps into it.
19. The Constitution will have life and respect only when the leaders of that country implement the spirit it represents.
20. The strongest governments in the world have the strongest network of secret service.
21. To preserve power, one should keep the minds of people busy and ensure that the gap between the rich and the poor never becomes huge.
22. If big countries sneeze, smaller countries catch cold. This is globalization redefined.
23. Corporate dictatorship is the new world order.
24. Democracy serves as a veil for corporate dictatorship.
25. The people who know too much about you are your biggest threat.
26. A person in power has more threat from his supporters than from his opponents.
27. Power is not a luxury. It's a responsibility.
28. When you are in power, you like to control. When you are not in power, you hate to be controlled.
29. Retaining power is as challenging as acquiring it.

30. Better to rule in hell than to serve in heaven.
31. An intellectual can influence millions. The mind of an intellectual is more powerful than an atom bomb.
32. If you have money power, you can acquire muscle power. If you have muscle power, you can acquire money power. Both money power and muscle power are complementary.
33. Power and wealth are complementary.
34. Every organization has two wings – intellectual wing and action wing. Intellectual wing plans everything and the action wing executes everything.
35. If the lawmakers become the law breakers, then it's time for a new power to replace them.
36. Few people cause immense suffering to many in the process of holding control.
37. Financial might and political might are complimentary. Both are needed to exercise absolute might.
38. Chaos immediately prevails after the death of a great ruler.
39. Even an enemy can be pardoned but not the guy who cheats.
40. One can tolerate an enemy but not the one who cheats.
41. Language unification can help in national integration.
42. History is all about the will of a man trying to gain control over other men.

43. Before you think of attack, be prepared to defend yourself.
44. Heads of nations are marketing agents of corporations.
45. Politicians can use power either to serve their self-interests or to serve people's interests.
46. Those who cannot be defeated by strength, should be defeated by using tact.
47. Without the fear of punishment, one cannot ensure discipline in society.
48. Punish few and create fear among millions from committing crimes.
49. Politicians are actors. Bureaucrats are directors. Corporate houses are producers and people are the audience.
50. If your enemy is silent, it doesn't mean that he is inactive.
51. Sustainable rulership lies in timely prediction and elimination of impending threats.
52. A person is called God, when he uses his might for the welfare of the people. A person is called a demon when he uses his might to suppress people.
53. Various ways to attain Salvation/Moksha/God - Some try to attain it by chanting the name of God. Some, by helping others. Some try to attain it by meditating in silence and staying aloof from the crowd. Some try to attain it by performing rituals. Some try to attain it by conducting themselves in an honest manner. Some try to attain it by fighting

against injustice. Some try to attain it by destroying those who are evil. Paths may be different but the destination is the same.

54. One should attack only when one has the capacity to defend.
55. Religious and ideological fanaticism swallow nations.
56. Ideas are more dangerous than bombs.
57. Fathers of girls look at the earning potential of the guys and political parties look at the spending potential of the candidates.
58. Rules don't apply to rulers.
59. There is no point in having rules when they are not implemented.
60. Without financial resources, no revolution can sustain.
61. Financial crimes have a larger impact compared to physical crimes.
62. Politicians derive their mileage out of the differences in public opinion.
63. Most unlucky countries in the world are landlocked countries.
64. If everyone wants to be the King, then who is going to be the soldier?
65. A disciplined army of few can overthrow an undisciplined army of many.
66. A soldier gets ready to sacrifice his life only when he is guaranteed that the welfare of his family will be undertaken by the organization for which he works.

67. Remaining dormant doesn't mean accepting defeat. It means, waiting for an opportunity to strike.
68. We need power to deliver justice. We need affluence to help those in need.
69. State alone cannot solve all the problems. Participation of people is equally important.
70. Constitutions aim at upholding individual's liberty but not at the cost of society.
71. One should join an organization by seeing its ideology but not the opportunity being provided by it.
72. We need institutions of power to serve the public at large in an organized manner.
73. The war happens inside before it happens outside.
74. A person gets attracted to a particular "ism"... Conflicts happen when a believer of one "ism" doesn't respect the existence and importance of other "isms"
75. Power and wealth lose relevance when they are acquired by exploiting others.
76. Differences are created among people to capture power.
77. Power loses its relevance when it is not used for the benefit of mankind.
78. Wars are created to gain control over the resources.
79. Wars are won and lost in the mind.
80. Armies indulge in direct wars whereas corporations indulge in proxy wars.

ENTREPRENEURSHIP

1. In the process of adding value to the world, you in turn become valuable.
2. Any business that is going to make people independent will thrive.
3. Entrepreneurs always play the game they think they are going to win.
4. Making money is the byproduct of doing something that we are passionate about. It's never a goal in itself.
5. I don't want to hear any hindrances. I want to hear only opportunities.
6. If you don't try now, you cannot try forever.
7. Time and opportunity don't wait for us.
8. When you find a way to change the lives of a billion people through your business, you become a billionaire by default.
9. It's up to us to create our opportunities and make use of them to the maximum extent.
10. Entrepreneurs see what others fail to see; entrepreneurs believe what others disbelieve; entrepreneurs try what others fail to try.
11. Becoming an entrepreneur is one of the biggest services to the world as entrepreneurs create employment, infrastructure and wealth.
12. There are a hell lot of opportunities lying around you. You should be open to them, grab them and write your own story.

13. All the progress in this world happens due to unconventional thinkers.
14. Everyone knows about the problems. People are looking for solutions. So we need to talk about solutions and not about problems.
15. A pessimistic person sees hurdles at every opportunity. An optimistic person sees opportunity in every hurdle.
16. There are three steps to become rich – make money, save money, invest and grow money.
17. Empowering the poor is better than feeding them.
18. Feeding makes people inefficient whereas empowering people makes them self-sufficient.
19. If you run after money, you can never catch it. If you run after your passion, money runs after you.
20. In the initial days, we take risks to grow in life. But after attaining the growth, we refrain from taking risks in the fear of losing the acquired growth.
21. Entrepreneurs need to innovate on a continuous basis to thrive in business.
22. Entrepreneurs are thrown out of business if they fail to innovate and change with the changing times.
23. Mind is the factory where ideas are manufactured.
24. Entrepreneurship is all about empowering people but not about overpowering them.
25. The wealth we create has no meaning if it doesn't bring about a positive transformation to society.

26. Jobs always limit the scope of an individual whereas entrepreneurship expands the scope of an individual.
27. I am not interested in money. I am interested in the freedom that comes by having abundance of it.

COURAGE & FEAR

1. Fear never finds place in the heart of a person who follows his conscience.
2. There is no place for excuse, no place for weakness and no place for impossibility.
3. The more you fear, the more you will be subjected to it. There is no bigger instrument of control bigger than fear.
4. The only thing that keeps holding you back from achieving what you intend to is your fear.
5. A man without attachments is the man without fear.
6. There is no disease bigger than fear.
7. Guilt, shame and fear of failure prevent a person from doing what they intend to.
8. Greed and fear are two most powerful emotions that are used to exploit anyone.
9. Fear keeps one away from living life to its fullest potential.
10. The happiest state of mind is fearlessness.
11. Fear destroys you whereas courage builds you.
12. A person who doesn't have the courage to follow his heart is considered to be dead though he is alive.
13. Step ahead to stand ahead.
14. If you don't have the courage to stand up for what you want, you are mentally dead though you are physically alive.
15. Don't be afraid of committing mistakes. It's not the loss that one should fear... it's not trying that one

should fear the most.

16. It is better to live without fear at least for a second rather than to live with fear for 100 years.
17. A man with fear has no place even in hell.
18. A bad guy with courage is better than a good guy with fear.
19. You are committing a bigger sin by remaining silent when injustice is happening in front of you than the person committing injustice.
20. Courage is life and fear is death.
21. Fear vanishes when what you say and do are one and the same.
22. For vision to become a reality, it takes a huge amount of time. In the meantime, one ought to have patience and courage.
23. The person who possesses both awareness and detachment is the one without fear.
24. People who lack the courage to take risks express their insecurity by talking about job security.
25. The more we fear, the more we are suppressed.
26. Courage is the asset which is the source to all other assets.
27. A person is said to be defeated only when he accepts defeat mentally. Till then, he remains undefeated.
28. An uneducated courageous person is better than an educated coward.
29. The harder the path, the tougher one becomes.
30. Courage and sound health are invaluable assets.
31. An opponent can dominate your mind if you have

fear.

32. Fear of social rejection compels one to act against one's conscience.
33. One should get used to rejection to emerge successful.
34. An indomitable will is needed to succeed in any endeavor.
35. A person is considered to be strong if he has conviction.
36. One needs to be physically fit and mentally tough.
37. Not fearing failure is the prerequisite to succeed.
38. You need to keep going even if you fall or fail. You need to just keep going. There is no other option. You need to just keep going till you win.
39. No one cares about the reasons or excuses you give to support your bullshit. All that matters is success and nothing else.
40. Courage is the bomb that reduces the fortifications of fear to ashes.
41. One who knows the truth, fears none.
42. Courage is the vaccine to get rid of the disease called fear.
43. Courage and confidence are evident in the eyes of the man who has acquired true knowledge.
44. Darkness cannot stop a man who wishes to march ahead.
45. The person who detaches himself from everything is the most fearless person.
46. Will power is the source to all other powers.

47. Don't think about the depth of the river when you decide to cross it... when you decide to do something, just do it.
48. The will to succeed transcends all limitations and obstacles.
49. When death is definite, why should you fear it?
50. One should not be afraid of taking risks. One should be afraid of not taking any risks.
51. Not taking risk is the biggest risk.
52. Death is the boon for those who are unable to live.
53. Don't be depressed when you fail and don't be proud when you win.

~~~~
~~~~